Are jellyfish made of jelly?

DK Direct Limited
Managing Art Editor Eljay Crompton
Senior Editor Rosemary McCormick
Writer Alexandra Parsons
Illustrators The Alvin White Studios and Richard Manning
Designers Wayne Blades, Veneta Bullen, Richard Clemson,
Sarah Goodwin, Diane Klein, Sonia Whillock

ISBN:1-56326-216-9

Contents

Are all sharks dangerous?

There are around 375 different kinds of sharks, and most of them are dangerous to other fish. Only about 30 types of them are dangerous to people. But to be on the safe side, never swim with sharks.

Hello, handsome!
The hammerhead shark is one of the strangest looking fish in the sea. Look how far apart its eyes are!

Chomp, chomp!
What do you get if you cross a shark with a helicopter?
A helichomper!

Look out!
Lifeguards are always on the lookout for that tell-tale fin! They are usually in radio contact with helicopter patrols just in case sharks are spotted close to the beach.

Big and small

☞ The whale shark is the biggest fish in the sea. A fully-grown one is bigger than two elephants. But don't worry, it only eats tiny little fish and shrimps!

☞ Some of the smallest kinds of sharks are only as long as your hand.

What did fish look like long ago?

Some looked like this coelacanth (SEE-le-canth), which was thought to have disappeared, just like dinosaurs, millions of years ago. Then one day in 1938, just off the coast of Africa, some fishermen found one in their nets. Since then several more have been seen swimming in the ocean.

Part of the family
The lungfish is related to the coelacanth. It's called a lungfish, because unlike most fish, it has lungs.

Where's the evidence?
People knew about coelacanths long before they saw them because they found fossils like this one. This fossil is 150 million years old.

Fishy facts

☞ The coelacanth is just over five feet long. That's about as long as a couch.

☞ The oldest fish fossil is about 470 million years old.

☞ The Australian lungfish uses its fins to crawl around under the water.

Are jellyfish made of jelly?

No. But in their bodies there is a layer of see-through wobbly material that looks a little like jelly. And that's how they get their name. There are many different kinds of jellyfish. They can be as small as a pea, or as large as a dining-room table. Most of them have tentacles with a nasty sting and none of them has a brain. Oh well!

Jelly family

The Portuguese man-of-war looks like a jellyfish, acts like a jellyfish, but isn't a jellyfish. Each one is really a colony of tiny sea creatures, called polyps. The polyps have their own special jobs to do. Some form tentacles and sting, some form a balloon and float, some feed, some swim, and some wobble!

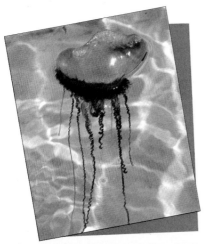

How many pounds?
Where are whales weighed?
In a whaleweigh station!

Whale feeding facts

☞ The blue whale eats up to four tons of food every day. Four tons is about the weight of 16,000 packed lunches. Imagine eating 16,000 packed lunches every day!

This blue whale is the largest animal on Earth – it weighs as much as 20 elephants.

11

Are there flowers in the ocean?

No, but there are little ocean creatures that look just like flowers. They are called sea anemones (a-NEM-o-nees). They are little tubes with a crown of pretty waving tentacles that look like petals.

Underwater garden
A coral reef is made up of tiny colorful animals called coral polyps that have a hard chalky outer shell. At night, the coral polyps poke out their tentacles to feed.

12

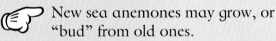

Pretty flowers
There are anemones in gardens and parks, too! They're not sea anemones though. They are pretty flowers that belong to the buttercup family.

Pretty things

 New sea anemones may grow, or "bud" from old ones.

Anemones catch tiny sea creatures in their stinging tentacles.

The one little fish an anemone doesn't eat is the clownfish. That's because the clownfish hides among the anemone's tentacles and keeps it clean.

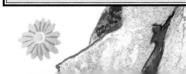

Is a sea horse really a horse?

Well, you just have to look at one to know! It has a head like a horse. But of course it isn't a horse. In fact, it has a tail like a monkey, a pouch like a kangaroo, and a hard outer layer like an insect. But a sea horse is really a fish. Most are tiny – about the size of your little finger.

14

Rocking horse

A mother sea horse lays her eggs in the father sea horse's pouch. He takes care of the eggs, and when the little ones hatch, the father rocks back and forth to help them get out of the pouch.

Tube head

The head of the sea horse ends in a long snout with a flap on the end that works like a trap door. The flap opens and the sea horse sucks in its dinner of tiny shrimp and fish eggs.

Sea horsey facts

 There are about 25 different types of sea horses in the world.

 There is one sea horse that can grow to be 12 inches long – the same size as a ruler.

 The sea horse has scales on the outside of its body which act like a kind of armor.

Are there forests in the ocean?

There aren't forests of trees, but there are "forests" of seaweeds. Just like trees on land, seaweeds are home to all kinds of critters. And just like trees, they give out oxygen, a gas that all creatures need.

What, no roots!
Seaweeds don't need roots to suck up water because their water supply is all around them! Seaweeds fix on to rocks with a bunch of little "suction cups" called holdfasts.

Gas bubbles
Like all plants, seaweeds need sunlight. Some seaweeds have gas-filled swellings on their fronds to keep them floating near the sunny surface of the water.

Weedy facts
 One of the largest plants on Earth is a seaweed. It is a giant kelp which can grow to 200 feet. That's about as tall as 33 grown-ups standing on each other's shoulders.

Which animals fly underwater?

Rays and skates do. They have very flat bodies and wing-like fins. They skim along the ocean bed, digging up shellfish for their supper. Some rays, like the manta ray and the eagle ray, are a little more energetic. They swim up near the surface and even leap out of the water from time to time.

18

Breathing problem

All fish need the oxygen in water to stay alive. Rays breathe through openings on the top of their head where water can come in and wash over their gills. Their gills collect oxygen.

Zooming along!
What's the fastest thing in the water?
A motor-pike!

Ray facts

☞ Electric rays are shocking! They catch their prey by zapping them with a sharp electric shock.

☞ Manta rays are the biggest rays. They can measure 23 feet from wingtip to wingtip. That's the length of a power boat.

Which are the nosiest fish?

The ones with the longest "noses"! Swordfish and sawfish have long, flattened upper jaws that look like a saw. The jaws have sharp edges and are about half as long as the fish's body. Swordfish can swim as fast as 60 mph, and there are stories that they have sliced boats in half!

Ouch!
A marlin is part of the swordfish family. It uses its saw-toothed snout as a weapon, sometimes stabbing its prey.

Swordfish facts

☞ Sawfish stay deep down in the ocean during the day, and come closer to the surface at night to feed.

☞ Swordfish like to eat squid, herring, and mackerel.

Are there snakes in the ocean?

Yes, there are. Most sea snakes have bodies which are flattened sideways. When they swim along they look like waving ribbons in the water. They glide just under the surface, breathing air through the nostrils on top of their head.

Deadly snake
This banded sea snake is very, very poisonous. It lives in the waters around Australia.

Fearful sight

There is a story told long ago of a terrible monster called Medusa who had snakes on her head instead of hair. She was so frightening to look at, that those who caught a glimpse of her were turned to stone.

Underwater snake facts

 Some sea snakes slither onto the beach to lay their eggs.

The largest sea snakes are up to 10 feet long. That's about as long as six classroom desks in a row.

W hich fish goes fishing?

The anglerfish. Anglerfish live in the deep, dark parts of the ocean where there is no sunlight. They have enormous jaws and pointy teeth, and a glowing "bait" that hangs down in front of their large mouth. The "bait" is really a tiny piece of flesh which some fish mistake for a tasty worm. When they try to grab it – that's the end of them.

Who's the boss?

There are many different types of anglerfish. The male anglerfish is a tiny little thing compared to the female. And what is more, some male anglerfish have no fishing pole of their own.

Fishy facts

☞ Deep-sea anglerfish are transparent – that means you can see right through them. Well, there's no point being colorful if you live in the dark!

Gone fishing

People who fish with a hook and a line are called anglers. They sometimes compete to see who can catch the biggest fish.

How do we keep the ocean clean?

The best way is for the nations of the world to stop using the oceans as a garbage dump. Governments have passed laws to stop the dumping of oil and chemical waste. But we can all do something to help, too. We can make sure we don't throw trash into the oceans and rivers.

Cleaning up oil

Sometimes giant tankers accidentally spill oil into the ocean, causing the water to become polluted. It is difficult to clean the oil up. Sometimes it can be sucked back up into tankers. If the oil is near the shore, detergents are used to clean up the mess.

To the rescue!

If sea birds get covered in oil, they can't fly or swim. Caring people rescue them and give them a bath.

Ways to help the ocean

☞ The plastic rings that hold soda cans together can be harmful to marine life. So remember to snip them before you put them in the garbage.

☞ It is best to take paper and cans to recycling centers. This way they won't end up in landfills, or in the ocean.

Mickey would like you to help him clean up the ocean.
Find the things that don't belong on the shore or in the ocean.